THE Prayers

OF

CHARLES R. SWINDOLL

VOLUME I

DEVOTIONAL PRAYERS ON 31 THEMES

INSIGHT FOR LIVING

The Prayers of Charles R. Swindoll, Volume 1
Devotional Prayers on 31 Themes

From the Bible-Teaching Ministry of Charles R. Swindoll

Charles R. Swindoll has devoted his life to the clear, practical teaching and application of God's Word and His grace. A pastor at heart, Chuck has served as senior pastor to congregations in Texas, Massachusetts, and California. He currently pastors Stonebriar Community Church in Frisco, Texas, but Chuck's listening audience extends far beyond a local church body. As a leading program in Christian broadcasting, *Insight for Living* airs in major Christian radio markets around the world, reaching people groups in languages they can understand. Chuck's extensive writing ministry has also served the body of Christ worldwide and his leadership as president and now chancellor of Dallas Theological Seminary has helped prepare and equip a new generation for ministry. Chuck and Cynthia, his partner in life and ministry, have four grown children and ten grandchildren.

Published By:
IFL Publishing House
A Division of Insight for Living
Post Office Box 251007
Plano, Texas 75025-1007

Editor in Chief: Cynthia Swindoll, President, Insight for Living
Executive Vice President: Wayne Stiles, Th.M., D.Min., Dallas Theological Seminary
Compiler: Derrick G. Jeter, Th.M., Dallas Theological Seminary
Content Editor: Amy L. Snedaker, B.A., English, Rhodes College
Copy Editors: Jim Craft, M.A., English, Mississippi College
    Kathryn Merritt, M.A., English, Hardin-Simmons University
Project Coordinator, Creative Ministries: Melanie Munnell, M.A., Humanities,
    The University of Texas at Dallas
Project Coordinator, Communications: Sarah Magnoni, A.A.S.,
    University of Wisconsin
Proofreader: Paula McCoy, B.A., English, Texas A&M University-Commerce
Cover Design: Kari Pratt, B.A., Commercial Art, Southwestern Oklahoma State University
Production Artist: Nancy Gustine, B.F.A., Advertising Art, University North Texas

ISBN: 978-1-57972-876-2
Printed in the United States of America

TABLE OF CONTENTS

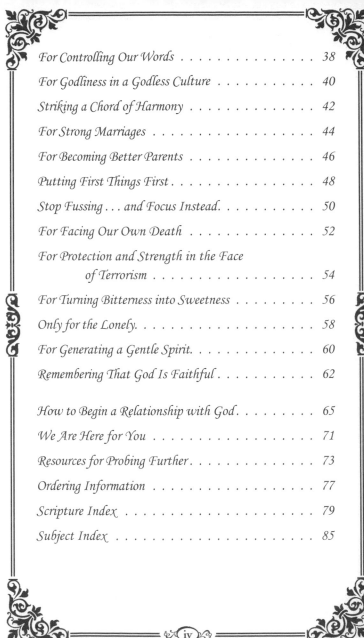

A LETTER FROM CHUCK

After more than four decades of ministry, I've come to the conclusion that prayer is the easiest and, at the same time, the hardest thing a follower of Christ can do. Easy because it involves something we do every day: talking. That's what prayer is, talking with God. J. Oswald Sanders, in his wonderful book *Spiritual Leadership*, wrote, "Prayer is the most ancient, most universal, most intensive expression of the religious instinct. It touches infinite extremes, for it is at once the simplest form of speech that infant lips can try and the sublimest strains that reach the Majesty on high. It is indeed the Christian's vital breath and native air."[1]

So why, then, is prayer so difficult? Why do we find it hard to "breathe"? Perhaps some of us are too lazy or impatient. Others of us are too embarrassed or ashamed to speak to the Lord of the universe, thinking our piddling problems too insignificant to bother Him. For many, and let's be honest here, prayer seems like we're only talking to air or whispering in an empty room. We know God is present and hears our prayers, yet there is that strange feeling of distance or isolation. Also, many of us find it hard to articulate what is within the depths of our hearts.

In spite of these struggles, let me encourage you to keep praying. Please use the book you hold in your hands to help you put into words what your heart and soul are trying to say to the Lord. These prayers, culled from years of ministry experience, are offered not because

I consider myself eloquent but in hopes that they might minister to you in your need. I encourage you to do more than just read them—make them your own.

Divided into thirty-one themes, these prayers cover the spectrum of life, from death to grace to marriage to temptation to terrorism. Every prayer is theologically sound, scripturally supported, and down-to-earth practical. Ideally, you'll find that these prayers enhance your quiet moments with the Master.

As you peruse these pages, may you find the lungs of your prayer life beginning to fill with ever deepening and refreshing air. May you discover that J. Oswald Sanders was right, prayer is the "Christian's vital breath and native air." So breathe . . . deeply, as you spend time in the clean air surrounding those special occasions of intimacy with the Majesty on high.

Charles R. Swindoll

---

1. J. Oswald Sanders, *Spiritual Leadership* (Chicago: Moody, 1980), 103.

THE
Prayers
OF
CHARLES R. SWINDOLL

Devote

yourselves to

prayer,

keeping alert

in it with an

attitude of

thanksgiving.

—Colossians 4:2

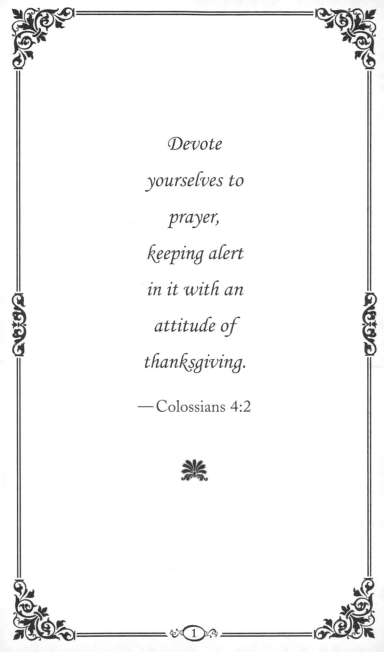

THE IMPORTANCE OF PRAYER

"O Lord, I beseech You, may Your ear be attentive to the prayer of Your servant and the prayer of Your servants who delight to revere Your name, and make Your servant successful today and grant him compassion before this man."

—Nehemiah 1:11

Father in heaven, we call upon You today. We know that You are the Giver of all good things . . . and that You never change like shifting shadows. We believe that Your heart is moved when Your people pray. So remind us, our Father, as we bow before You, that there is nothing more important we can do when facing situations that are beyond us . . . than to pray.

We remember that prayer forces us to wait, and we must learn to wait patiently for Your timing. Prayer quiets our hearts before You. The chaos subsides and life seems to settle down around us as we pray. Prayer clears our vision, Father, as we think about our lives, as we ponder where we're going, and as we pursue Your will. May we walk with You in such a way that our obedience is revealed through deeds that honor Your name . . . even when that means doing the hard things You want us to do.

For those who are in a difficult strait, under pressure, up against a wall, facing a test—perhaps the greatest in their lives—we ask that You remind them that the saint who advances on his or her knees never retreats. Help them remember that You are still on Your throne and they are still at Your footstool . . . with only a knee's distance between the two of you.

May we all become people who pray. May we also learn to leave the burden with You, rather than pick it up and carry it with us after claiming that we're trusting You. Right now, Lord, take the burden. We cast it upon You, knowing that You're better able to handle it than we ever will be. We ask that this time of prayer might make a difference in the balance of this day . . . which we commit to You now, in the name of Jesus, our Savior. Amen.

See also Psalm 40:1; Mark 1:35 – 39; 1 Timothy 2:1; James 1:17; 5:13; 1 Peter 5:7.

For Growing toward Maturity

Summing up: Be agreeable, be sympathetic, be loving, be compassionate, be humble. That goes for all of you, no exceptions. No retaliation. No sharp-tongued sarcasm. Instead, bless—that's your job, to bless. You'll be a blessing and also get a blessing.

Whoever wants to embrace life
*   and see the day fill up with good,*
Here's what you do:
*   Say nothing evil or hurtful;*
Snub evil and cultivate good;
*   run after peace for all you're worth.*
God looks on all this with approval,
*   listening and responding well to what*
*   he's asked;*
But he turns his back
*   on those who do evil things.*

—1 Peter 3:8–12 MSG

Father, thank You for the reminder of character qualities that are such a vital part of our Christian lives. Though we bear very few of the marks of maturity Peter wrote about in the passage above, we always need to be stirred up by way of reminder. How often we have come before

You, asking for help in these areas! You have heard our pleas on many occasions. Truth be told, You will hear them again. We yearn to be like Your Son, Jesus, the One who modeled each of these marks of maturity to perfection, though fully man. We long to grow in spiritual maturity . . . but the uphill journey takes so long. We confess that it often feels unending.

Thank You for the promise that Your Holy Spirit will be with us each step of the way. We desperately need His empowerment to keep us going and growing . . . until we become like Jesus . . . fully conformed to His image.

We ask, Father, that You give us hope beyond our immaturity. Help us in our unbelief. Guard us from discouragement. As we look back over the checklist You gave to Peter—and realize how far we have to go—remind us also how far we've come, by Your grace. Remind us that You will complete the good work You began in us . . . until the day of Christ Jesus.

Through His matchless name we pray. Amen.

See also John 14:16–17; Galatians 5:16;
Philippians 1:6; Hebrews 5:8; 2 Peter 1:13.

FOR DAILY DOUBTS

He said to Thomas, "Reach here with your finger, and see My hands; and reach here your hand and put it into My side; and do not be unbelieving, but believing." Thomas answered and said to Him, "My Lord and my God!"

—John 20:27–28

Our Father, encourage us—especially we who often doubt and feel ashamed of our doubt. May we realize that You are in the midst of our reflections and, through such inner searching, we can come to new insights and deeper depths that otherwise we would never have known.

Thank You for preserving the story of Thomas. We see ourselves portrayed so vividly in his doubts. May we come to a realization that You're pleased even in our searching, and You honor our honest questions. Thank You for accepting us in our struggles and understanding our doubts. Thank You for Your grace in understanding that though we weep when we lose our friends and family, and we question the tragedies and calamities of life, it isn't that we doubt Your right to rule. It's that we struggle with releasing our own rights . . . we're simply trying to reason our way through those mysterious valleys.

Father, we wish to know You as we've never known You before. May today be the beginning of increasing trust and decreasing doubts.

We ask this in the rock-solid name of Jesus, our Lord and our God. Amen.

See also Matthew 14:28–33; James 1:5–8; Jude 1:22.

FIGHTING FOR THE TRUTH

Shadrach, Meshach and Abed-nego replied to the king, "O Nebuchadnezzar, we do not need to give you an answer concerning this matter. If it be so, our God whom we serve is able to deliver us from the furnace of blazing fire; and He will deliver us out of your hand, O king. But even if He does not, let it be known to you, O king, that we are not going to serve your gods or worship the golden image that you have set up."

—Daniel 3:16–18

Our Father in heaven, as a result of Your Word we pray that You might grant to us insight into our homes, our nation, and this world. We ask You to raise up from this world that is given to passivity and compromise a body of people who will live for and, if necessary, fight for the truth. We pray that we might not embrace the false philosophies of our day, which sound so logical and appealing but in the end turn us into passive fools. We pray, our Father, that we might become balanced believers, that we might discern times in which it is necessary to be very still and quiet; times in which it is essential to say, "Lord, this is Your battle. Please, You take this for me"; and other times when the issue is such that we say,

"Even if I must stand alone, I will stand. Even if it means I will be beaten to the death, I will take that, because an issue greater than all is at stake."

Thank You for the reminder of those women and men in uniform who fight courageously so that we might enjoy the quietness of this moment and the freedom of public worship. Father, steel us. Put strength and integrity where there has been weakness. Replace the flab and the fat of our day with the muscle of conviction. And, Lord, may it come to pass that You raise up from our homes a body of young people who have convictions that reach deeper than any persuasive word of the world. If You will do this, our Father, we will be eternally grateful. Through Christ we pray. Amen.

See also Ecclesiastes 3:3, 8;
1 Corinthians 1:20–21; 3:19; 2 Timothy 2:3–4;
James 4:17.

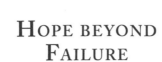

Hope beyond
Failure

Just as he was speaking, the rooster crowed. The Lord turned and looked straight at Peter. Then Peter remembered the word the Lord had spoken to him: "Before the rooster crows today, you will disown me three times." And [Peter] went outside and wept bitterly.

—Luke 22:60–62 NIV

Dear Father, every one of us has experienced failure. *Many* failures. They have left us broken, depressed, disappointed in ourselves, and full of regret. There are times when flashbacks of those episodes return to haunt us. How distressed we can feel in those moments! Thank You for the remarkable transformation made possible by forgiveness. Thank You for understanding that we are but dust, often incapable of keeping our own promises or living up to our own expectations.

Renew our hope as we reflect on Peter, with whom we can so easily identify. Remind us that, just as You used him after his failures, You will also use us, by Your grace. In fact, help our memories of failure bring about a humility that sees Your grace as it really is . . . *amazing*.

Help us find fresh encouragement and new strength from Your Word. We look to You alone for the ability to hope again. Only You have the power to make something beautiful and good out of lives that are littered with the debris of thoughts we should never have entertained . . . words we should never have said . . . and deeds we should never have done.

Our only source of relief comes through Your grace. Bring it to our attention again and again in those critical moments when discouragement does a number on us . . . and make us grateful.

In the gracious name of Jesus we ask this. Amen.

See also Psalm 32:1–11; Micah 7:19; John 21:15–19; Romans 8:28.

Courage for the Discouraged

I waited patiently for the Lord;
And He inclined to me and heard my cry.
He brought me up out of the pit of
destruction, out of the miry clay,
And He set my feet upon a rock making my
footsteps firm.

—Psalm 40:1–2

Lord, we pray that You would bring relief when we are swamped with the ever-rising tide of discouragement. Grant deliverance for us who are caught in that swamp and start to slide into its slimy waters. Encourage our hearts as we face those depressing, dark moments that leave us feeling hopeless and believing the lie that things will never change. Father, give us hope beyond the heartbreaks we experience. We cling to the inspired words of the apostle Peter that if we humble ourselves before the mighty hand of God, You will lift us up. You *will* exalt us at the proper time. Discouragement keeps us humble, we confess, for we are never discouraged and bigheaded at the same time.

In humbleness, Father, we call upon You as Your children. We ask You to lift our spirits by transforming our minds. Strengthen us to see the value of dwelling on things that are true, honest, just, pure, lovely, and of good report. Help us to fix our minds on heavenly things rather than on those earthly things that drag us down.

Give us a rallying point around Your grace, dear Lord. We need that point of focus, our times being as they are . . . and our moods so given to change. Thank You that Christ loves us and keeps on loving us. Thank You that while we were yet sinners, Christ died for us. Thank You that the grace that saved us keeps us saved . . . regardless of our doubts and other weird feelings.

We also pray for those weary souls who have never met Your Son as Savior. How do they ever make it through the day? We ask that their burden of discouragement would be lifted by the realization that Jesus's death on the cross paid the complete price for their sins. Help them see past their pain to the reality that there is nothing they need to do or promise or change or give up or become . . . in order to be accepted by You. Help them to trust in Your Son. May they do so today.

Now to Him who is able to guard us from stumbling and to cause us to stand in the presence of His glory blameless with great joy, to the only God our Savior . . . be glory, majesty, dominion, and authority . . . now and forever.

In His great name we pray. Amen.

See also Psalm 69:1–4; Daniel 4:36–37; Acts 16:31;
Romans 5:8; 12:2; Philippians 4:8; Colossians 3:1–4;
1 Peter 5:6; Jude 1:24–25.

FINDING JUSTICE IN INJUSTICE

And I saw something else under the sun:
In the place of judgment — wickedness was
*   there,*
in the place of justice — wickedness was there.
I thought in my heart,
"God will bring to judgment both the righteous
*   and the wicked,*
for there will be a time for every activity,
*   a time for every deed."*

— Ecclesiastes 3:16–17 NIV

It's not often, Father, that we make such a statement, but today we thank You for the injustices in life that have crippled us and broken us and crushed us. Unfair circumstances have bruised us deeply and beaten us into submission to You. Inequities have brought us to such a dead end that we can't see the way back out. The only direction we can look is up. We often think that our unjust circumstance is what has ruined our lives . . . when instead, it could be the means You have ordained to give us life. Father, if those people we know who have trudged through the valley of the shadow of death were not alive today, walking with You and telling us to keep going, where would we be? How much we need their examples and encouragement! Thank You for each one.

In light of Your sovereign grace, we thank You for blindness, for paralysis, for loss, for death, for broken dreams, for dissolved partnerships, and for disillusionment. In faith, we praise You for times of insecurity, failure, divorce, and even those when others have treated us unjustly. We see the storm, but You enable us to also see beyond the storm, so we trust You to make all things just in Your time. We believe that You sovereignly intend for good what others intentionally mean for evil.

We pray for those facing the frustration of injustice in these and dozens of other categories. We ask that they may be able to find in Jesus Christ the strength to go on . . . especially those who have almost decided to give up. We pray that they will offer everything to You in full surrender. Everything.

In the name of Jesus Christ, the Conqueror. Amen.

See also Genesis 50:20; Psalm 23:4; Psalm 119:71; Ecclesiastes 3:11; Romans 8:28; 2 Corinthians 1:3–7.

HONORING GOD'S SOVEREIGNTY

"His dominion is an everlasting dominion,
And His kingdom endures from generation to
generation.
All the inhabitants of the earth are accounted
as nothing,
But He does according to His will in the host
of heaven
And among the inhabitants of earth;
And no one can ward off His hand
Or say to Him, 'What have You done?'"

—Daniel 4:34–35

Sovereign God, all of us would be quick to say that we do need to be relieved of our anxieties—they are too many and too frequent. And because we want to call our own shots, we need to be leveled and removed from the realm of pride.

Help us stop feeling as though we need an explanation of why, as life unfolds around us. Show us again, Lord, that You are God and there is no other—that our God is in the heavens; He does whatever He pleases. You are at work in our lives, in the lives of our neighbors, in the lives of those who live across the street, across the country, and across the seas. You are at work. No one else is in charge, and You do all things well. You change the times and the seasons. You also change us.

Make Your Word as relevant as tomorrow morning's news on the Internet, as significant as what we would read in the daily paper. And bring us back to the recognition of Your sovereignty, Father: we answer to You because You are our all in all.

Today we worship Your Son as Lord, and we worship Your name as the one and only true God through whom, thankfully, we have a salvation that is eternal and secure. We rest in these truths as Your children.

We also remember those who have never met Your Son as Savior. Give them unrest, uneasiness, even sleepless nights until they find their peace and rest in knowing You . . . not in understanding their circumstances. May they believe in You through faith in Christ, in whose name we pray. Amen.

See also Genesis 50:20; Job 40:1–5; Psalm 115:3;
Romans 8:28; 9:20–21.

COMPASSION IN SUFFERING

He was despised and forsaken of men,
A man of sorrows and acquainted with grief;
And like one from whom men hide their face
He was despised, and we did not esteem Him.
Surely our griefs He Himself bore,
And our sorrows He carried;
Yet we ourselves esteemed Him stricken,
Smitten of God, and afflicted.

—Isaiah 53:3–4

Lord, words of hope from others can fall flat if things aren't right in our own lives. When we're consumed by rage and resentment, somehow words about joy and purpose sound hollow . . . they seem meaningless. But when our hearts are right with You, we have ears to hear the message of hope. Rather than resisting others' words, we appreciate them, and we love You for sending them to us in a time of need.

Father, truth be told, some of us are in great anguish. Give us grace to match our trials—better still, *to rise above* them. Grant a sense of hope and purpose beyond our pain. Bless us with a fresh reminder that we are not alone . . . that Your plan has not been thwarted . . . that we have not been abandoned even when our suffering gets worse, not better.

After You have strengthened us—and we are on our feet—help us maintain a compassion for those who suffer. Give us a listening ear and a word of encouragement for others living in this world of hurt. Remind us how we felt when we were there . . . and that Your plan for us may include another walk with You down the narrow and rugged path of suffering. And remind us also that Your Son, though sinless, was acquainted with grief.

We ask this in the compassionate name of the Man of Sorrows. Amen.

See also Proverbs 25:20; 2 Corinthians 1:3–7;
Hebrews 12:3; 1 Peter 2:21.

LEARNING HUMILITY

Clothe yourselves with humility toward one another, for God is opposed to the proud, but gives grace to the humble. Therefore humble yourselves under the mighty hand of God, that He may exalt you at the proper time.

—1 Peter 5:5–6

Father, we all have hopes and aspirations. We all have dreams. And though there is nothing wrong with these, how easy it is to be driven by them. How easy it is to feel that if our dreams don't come true, we've somehow not been loved by You. We've been trained to take care of ourselves—a fine idea that has gone to seed. It's all about *my* stuff, *my* rights, *my* promotion, *my* salary, *my* place, *my* name . . . how ugly! How unchristian. We acknowledge before You that this life is not about us or our expectations.

Thank You that You never miss a person. When it's time for promotion, You won't be late. When it's time for rewards, You won't forget. So, at this awesome moment, we bow before Your mighty throne. We acknowledge that You've been good to us when we've not deserved it. You've cared for us when we've been careless. You've loved us when we've been terribly unloving, and You've met our needs when we didn't even stop to think about what we ought to be giving to You and Your work. You faithfully and graciously and constantly pour out Your good things upon us. Thank You for Your deliverance. Thank You for Your discipline.

Teach us in these tender days the value of genuine humility—of a self-forgetful life. We ask this so that we might become for You messengers whose message makes sense because our lives are like Your Son's life—the One who is gentle and humble of heart.

We pray in His name, for His glory. Amen.

See also Matthew 11:29; 16:21–26; Luke 14:11; Philippians 2:3–8.

Overcoming Guilt by Remembering Whose We Are

For I am convinced that neither death, nor life, nor angels, nor principalities, nor things present, nor things to come, nor powers, nor height, nor depth, nor any other created thing, will be able to separate us from the love of God, which is in Christ Jesus our Lord.

—Romans 8:38–39

Dear gracious Father, we're our own worst enemy. We focus on our failures rather than on Your rescues. We remember our wrongs rather than rejoice in Your power to make us right. We rely on our puny efforts to get through the day rather than on Your sovereign plans for our ultimate good. Even our attempts at being devoted to You are all-too-often self-centered and self-serving. Turn our attention back to You.

Remind us of our exalted position in Christ—that You have qualified us to share in the inheritance of the saints in Light. Keep uppermost in our minds that You have rescued us from the domain of darkness and transferred us to the kingdom of Your beloved Son.

Refresh us with frequent flashbacks from Your inerrant and reliable Word. "If God is for us, who is against us? . . . Who will separate us from the love of Christ? Will tribulation, or distress, or persecution, or famine, or nakedness, or peril, or sword? . . . But in all these things we overwhelmingly conquer through Him who loved us."

Renew our spirits with the realization that we're Your possession—that we are a chosen race, a royal priesthood, a holy nation, a people for Your own possession.

Then, with those joyful thoughts to spur us on, slay the dragon of guilt within us so we might enjoy, as never before, Your comforting and reassuring embrace. Through Christ our conquering Savior we pray. Amen.

See also Psalm 51:10; Romans 8:31, 35, 37;
Colossians 1:12–13; 1 Peter 2:9.

FOR RELIEF
FROM SHAME

"If any one of you is without sin, let him be the first to throw a stone at her." Again he stooped down and wrote on the ground. At this, those who heard began to go away one at a time, the older ones first, until only Jesus was left, with the woman still standing there. Jesus straightened up and asked her, "Woman, where are they? Has no one condemned you?" "No one, sir," she said. "Then neither do I condemn you," Jesus declared. "Go now and leave your life of sin."

—John 8:7–11 NIV

We are grateful, Father, that Your Son did not come to call the righteous but sinners to repentance. By Your grace, You have invited people who are imperfect, who are sinful, who have every reason to be ashamed of themselves, who are failures, who are guilty of wrong, to come to You and to find in You relief from their burdens, hope beyond the present, and relief from shame.

Living in self-condemnation for something we have done wrong, we often forget, there is now no condemnation for those who are in Christ Jesus. So, this very moment we pray, Father, that You will bring to Yourself those who have not yet found a way to silence the accusers within them—the thoughts that condemn as judge and jury. The tragedy is, when we hear those thoughts, we believe them as true! Give us the first of several steps toward relief. Today, we come to the One who is qualified to judge and condemn but, because of His death and resurrection, has set us free. May we find ultimately the joy of living by grace because of the finished work of Jesus Christ our Savior.

In Jesus's name we pray. Amen.

See also Zephaniah 3:19; Luke 5:32;
Romans 8:1, 33 – 34.

FOR VICTORY OVER TEMPTATION

No temptation has overtaken you but such as is common to man; and God is faithful, who will not allow you to be tempted beyond what you are able, but with the temptation will provide the way of escape also, so that you will be able to endure it.

—1 Corinthians 10:13

Thank You, Father, for Your penetrating truth preserved through the centuries. Thank You for the careful concern of men like the apostles Peter and Paul who knew both sides of life on planet Earth: what it was like to live in this old world and what it was like to walk with the Savior, Your Son. Thank You for Peter's admonishment to prepare our minds for action, to keep sober in spirit, to fix our hope on Your grace, and not to conform our lives to the former lusts . . . but . . . to be holy as You are. Thank You for Paul's confidence that You won't allow temptation to push us into an inescapable corner.

Lord, because You don't save us and then suddenly take us home to heaven but leave us here on earth, hear us as we ask You to bring to our attention those things that will assist us in staying clean in a corrupt world. Give us an intense distaste for things that displease You.

At the same time, give us a renewed pleasure in things that uphold Your honor and magnify Your truth. As You do this, we will have what we crave: victory over temptation.

We ask this in the name of Him who consistently and victoriously withstood the relentless blast of the Devil's temptations, Jesus our Lord. Amen.

See also Matthew 4:1–11; 1 Peter 1:13–16; 5:8–9; 2 Peter 2:9.

FOR PERSONAL INTEGRITY

From the care of the ewes with suckling lambs
He brought [David]
To shepherd Jacob His people,
And Israel His inheritance.
So he shepherded them according to the
integrity of his heart,
And guided them with his skillful hands.

—Psalm 78:71–72

Father, personal purity is never automatic or easily produced. Integrity doesn't flow from our flesh naturally or freely. In fact, many of us have lived too many days of our lives in hypocrisy and deception. That's why we need You so desperately. We don't know how to unravel the mess of our bad habits or untie the knots of our past, so we're tempted to continue ignoring Your convicting voice and living lives of regret. But enough is enough! We are determined to ignore it no longer. We refuse to wade any longer in shallow pools of carnality. Beginning today, we are determined to live lives of integrity. We ask You to honor our decision to walk with You, to cease our life of duplicity, to stop compromising our integrity. Give us Your strength, dear Father, Your help, Your courage, Your wisdom. Forgive our foolish and hypocritical ways. Deliver us from the dangerous and deep quicksand of deceitful sin and establish us on the solid rock of vulnerability and integrity.

May Your grace keep us from a judgmental spirit toward others, Lord. Give us the encouragement we need to be all You have called us to be as Your obedient children, so that we, like David with the sheep, might guide others skillfully and well.

In the strong name of Jesus Christ our Lord. Amen.

See also Job 8:20; Psalm 15:1–2;
Proverbs 2:6–7; 10:9; 20:7.

GRATITUDE FOR GRACE

For the grace of God has appeared, bringing salvation to all men, instructing us to deny ungodliness and worldly desires and to live sensibly, righteously and godly in the present age.

—Titus 2:11–12

Thank You, dear Lord, for the beautiful way You teach us. Thank You for Your patience when we fail. Thank You for Your understanding in the midst of all our own confusion. Thank You for reaching down to us when we would never have reached up to You. Thank You for stopping us when we were running in the wrong direction, for setting the hounds of heaven after us. Thank You especially for Your grace. For by grace we have been saved through faith; and that not of ourselves, it is the gift of God; not as a result of works, so that no one may boast. What a great reminder!

Thank You, dear God, for being tough with us when we needed it, for disciplining us so that we would walk worthy of the calling. How grateful we are that You have promised us a heavenly home free of guilt and shame and sin and sorrow and death. We look forward to eternity with You, with our Savior whom having not seen, we love; in whom, though now we see Him not, yet believing, we rejoice with joy unspeakable and full of glory.

In the great name of Jesus we thank You. Amen.

See also Psalm 84:10–11; John 1:16;
Ephesians 2:8–9; 1 Peter 1:8.

GUARDING AGAINST LEGALISM

Jesus said, "Get up, take your bedroll, start walking." The man was healed on the spot. He picked up his bedroll and walked off. That day happened to be the Sabbath. The Jews stopped the healed man and said, "It's the Sabbath. You can't carry your bedroll around. It's against the rules."... The man went back and told the Jews that it was Jesus who had made him well. That is why the Jews were out to get Jesus — because he did this kind of thing on the Sabbath.

—John 5:8–10, 15–16 MSG

Heavenly Father, it is our deep desire to glorify Your name. We want to honor Your Word, even when it squares off against our own feelings or experiences. We thank You for being kind enough to teach us the basic things about grace. And we pray that teaching might result in freedom from the bondage that has held captive some of Your people far too long.

Now we ask for several things — that You would guard us from extremism; that You would guard us from misunderstanding; that You would guard Your children from foolish, licentious living; and that You would guard us from a misappropriation of freedom. And, Father, that You would guard those of us who keep lists from thinking that our lists make us more holy. Deal first with our attitude, our Father, then with our lives — whether it's for salvation, or for deliverance from the terrible plague of legalism, or simply for the joy of living free in Christ.

We ask it in the name that is above all names, Jesus Himself. Amen.

See also Matthew 23:23; Galatians 5:1;
1 Peter 2:16.

OVERCOMING HYPOCRISY

"Be especially careful when you are trying to be good so that you don't make a performance out of it. It might be good theater, but the God who made you won't be applauding."

—Matthew 6:1 MSG

Lord God, we thank You for the model of Jesus Christ our Savior who, when He walked this earth, dripped with authenticity. We long to be authentic as our Savior was—not phony and proud and faking our commitment to You but people who have a faith that's genuine, not counterfeit. That takes courage. It takes guts to live the real life before a world that's lost its way, where hypocrisy is so often modeled and comes across as religious piety.

Forgive us, Father, for the way we have subtly sought the applause of others, hoping they'd be impressed with our humility or our generosity or even our authenticity, which wasn't authenticity at all. We pray that we'll be more effective in secret than we ever could be in public and that, as a result of Your seeing us in secret, You'll be honored and the rewards will come at a time when it's just between You and us.

Father, we pray that You will turn reproof into restoration and thereby change us so that we become like Christ—and unlike the Pharisees who were so impressed with themselves. May we instead be so impressed with You that we lose sight of ourselves. And in that self-forgetful state, may we give You all the glory that You deserve.

It is in the strong name of Jesus Christ that we pray. Amen.

See also Matthew 6:4–18; 23:13–51;
Romans 12:9; James 3:17; 1 Peter 2:1–2.

TRUTH TO LIVE BY, TRUTH TO DIE FOR

See how I love your precepts;
preserve my life, O LORD, according to
your love.
All your words are true;
all your righteous laws are eternal.

—Psalm 119:159–160 NIV

Thank You, Father, for breathing out Your Word through men so many centuries ago. Thank You for preserving the message that You revealed through the miracle of inspiration, Father. Thank You for Your Word—the inerrant, authoritative, infallible Word of God. We live in a day in which others' words have replaced your eternal Word, at least in the public's mind. In this difficult era, it is hard to hear again Your Word. We pray that the scales will be lifted from our eyes and that which has blocked our hearing will be removed so we might see and hear and be comforted and encouraged by Your revealed Word. May the truth that appears in Your Word make its journey through our minds and probe deep within our hearts, so that our minds are transformed and as a result, our actions.

Father, we pray that You will cause us to glean from Your Word truth to live by, knowing that it represents

truth to die for. Ours is a troubled era. The battle for men's and women's souls and for our youth's minds is raging. And rather than simply throwing a fit and screaming at the top of our voices, we bring our requests to You. We ask that Your truth may equip us with sufficient ammunition to do battle in a world that's lost its way and is guided by an enemy who is deceptive and effective, who knows exactly where he's going. We pray that we will grasp the value of doctrine as it establishes us for whatever comes our way—those surprises, those unexpected events, those things we will call tragedies, and those joys and delights that are before us.

Anchor us, our Father, to the bedrock of truth and remind us that Your Son, Jesus Christ, is the same yesterday and today and forever. It's all His story. Our Father, our eyes are upon Jesus. It is in His merciful, matchless name we pray. Amen.

❧

*See also Isaiah 40:6–8; John 17:17;
2 Timothy 3:16–17; Hebrews 13:8; 2 Peter 1:19–21.*

FOR CONTROLLING
OUR WORDS

See how great a forest is set aflame by such a small fire! And the tongue is a fire, the very world of iniquity; the tongue is set among our members as that which defiles the entire body, and sets on fire the course of our life, and is set on fire by hell.

—James 3:5–6

Our Father, our tongues are far too often wicked and out of control! We have breached confidences that were meant to be held in trust. We have told several people of the offense we received but have failed to speak with the offender to make things right. And we have spoken jealous and envious words of one who was promoted over us. Many lack the courage to tell us to our face of our error, but You don't; You command us to get control of our tongues. We're rebuked by Your indictment: from the same mouth come both blessing and cursing . . . these things ought not to be this way.

Lord, help us to remember that there's no decision more important than salvation. And on the heels of that, there's no decision more important than the decision to restore a relationship that has been fractured because of hurtful words. Forgive us for speaking before we knew the facts or before we earned the right to say what we've said. Forgive us for hurting a brother or a sister who wasn't even there to defend himself or herself. Hear our prayer today and vindicate us, Lord, for we, too, have been verbally assassinated and our integrity has been violated. And we ask You to fight our battles for us. We come to You today in faith in the name of Jesus Christ our Lord. And with our tongues we say, amen.

See also Psalm 120:1–4; Proverbs 16:27–28; James 3:8–12.

For Godliness in a Godless Culture

Don't you realize that this is not the way to live? Unjust people who don't care about God will not be joining in his kingdom. Those who use and abuse each other, use and abuse sex, use and abuse the earth and everything in it, don't qualify as citizens in God's kingdom. A number of you know from experience what I'm talking about, for not so long ago you were on that list. Since then, you've been cleaned up and given a fresh start by Jesus, our Master, our Messiah, and by our God present in us, the Spirit.

—1 Corinthians 6:9–11 MSG

Lord God, Your Son has closed yesterday's door, therefore Your people don't have to live enslaved to sin or shame anymore. Not because we've been strong and good and noble, but because You have transformed our lives. You've changed our course of direction. Even though You've left us on foreign soil, as aliens and strangers, we have a home in heaven. And sometimes we get pretty homesick!

Hear the prayers of Your people as we call out to You. Give us self-control on those occasions when we're tempted to moralize and put people down. Make us aware that a godly life preaches an unforgettable message to the unsaved. Help us remember that we're soldiers away from our home in heaven, living in a culture that's lost its way and is in desperate need of Jesus Christ. Keep us easy to live with, strong in faith, unbending in our convictions yet full of grace toward those who are bound by sin and captured by habits they cannot break. Enable us to shock this pagan culture with lives that are authentic, that stay balanced, that are still fun, and that ultimately glorify You, O God . . . just like Jesus did.

In His great name we pray. Amen.

See also John 15:18–19; 17:15–20;
Romans 12:1–2; 1 Peter 2:11.

STRIKING A CHORD
OF HARMONY

Therefore I, the prisoner of the Lord, implore you to walk in a manner worthy of the calling with which you have been called, with all humility and gentleness, with patience, showing tolerance for one another in love, being diligent to preserve the unity of the Spirit in the bond of peace.

—Ephesians 4:1–3

Lord, we realize that this is straight talk from You: "Preserve the unity of the Spirit in the bond of peace." It doesn't win votes, but it gets attention. It doesn't promise that we'll get our way, but it teaches truth. Your way is the best way . . . forbid that we ever go any other way. We've tried those ways. They're all dead-end streets or, if not that, they lead into dangerous swamps.

So we pray that You will give Your people a sense of recommitment to this matter of unity and harmony and confidentiality and purity and love and tolerance and patience through Your words, gentleness, humility, in the bond of peace. May we model that unity, Lord. May we model it when we're at home, when we're in our neighborhoods, when we're at our workplaces, when we're

behind the steering wheels of our cars, when we're doing business, when we're at the grocery store, when we're meeting new friends, and any other time we're given the opportunity to impact another life. Give us great harmony, Lord. As You grow us up, grow us deep. May our roots deepen as our fruit ripens.

Now unto Him who is able to keep us from falling, and to present us faultless before the presence of His glory with exceeding joy, to the only wise God our Savior, be glory and majesty, dominion and power, both now and forever.

In the name of Your dear Son. Amen.

See also Proverbs 10:11–12; John 13:34–35;
1 John 2:9–11; 4:7–9; Jude 1:24–25.

FOR STRONG MARRIAGES

Husbands, love your wives, just as Christ also loved the church and gave Himself up for her. . . . So husbands ought also to love their own wives as their own bodies. He who loves his own wife loves himself . . . and the wife must see to it that she respects her husband.

—Ephesians 5:25, 28, 33

Lord, today we are living in a culture that has forgotten Your pattern for marriage. The world has lost its way because Your Word is being ignored. We have gotten the threads of that divine tapestry all mixed up, and the whole thing is a mess. Furthermore, our culture is a total disaster. The fracturing of homes has become so commonplace that we no longer even raise our eyebrows when we hear of another family going under. We pray, therefore, that the truths of the words above, presented from Your exacting pattern, the Word of God, would find root and bear fruit in some lives. We also pray that You'd give husbands and wives the courage to say, "I am wrong. I am sorry. Please forgive me. Let's start over." We ask that You would give partners who hear those words a renewed capacity to believe their spouses, to work alongside them, to help make Your design a reality.

Thank You, Father, for Jesus, who is here for us, who loves us, and who modeled sacrificial love on our behalf. Help us, Lord, as we live out His life in our marriages through the enabling power of Your Spirit.

Through Christ our Lord, we pray. Amen.

See also Genesis 2:23–25; Mark 10:5–9;
1 Corinthians 7:1–9; Hebrews 13:4.

FOR BECOMING
BETTER PARENTS

Fathers, do not provoke your children to anger, but bring them up in the discipline and instruction of the Lord.

—Ephesians 6:4

Thank You, Father, for being the perfect Parent. Thank You for those times that You've taken us to task, though the reproof sometimes seemed more than we could bear. Encourage us with the truth that whoever the Lord loves He reproves, even as a father corrects the son in whom he delights. Forgive us, our Father, for our prodigal ways, for our selfish desires and self-willed decisions. Forgive us for our pride in wanting to look like winners as fathers and mothers when the truth is we have failed at every point.

Help us to be real with our children—authentic, loving, forgiving, firm when we have to be, strong when we need to be, gentle at all times. Help us, Lord. Help us with our grandchildren, to be there for them when they need us to be supportive and affirming of their parents, to be a part of the answer rather than a part of the problem. Enable us to come to terms with things that weren't dealt with in our own lives so that we don't pass them on to these precious, innocent children who follow us.

Lord, we give You thanks for the genius of the family. It's all Your idea. We pray we'll have very sensitive hearts as we grow in these areas of nurturing and discovery.

In the dear name of Christ. Amen.

See also Matthew 11:29; 16:21–26; Luke 14:11; Philippians 2:3 – 8.

PUTTING FIRST
THINGS FIRST

"No one can serve two masters; for either he will hate the one and love the other, or he will be devoted to one and despise the other. You cannot serve God and wealth. . . . But seek first His kingdom and His righteousness, and all these things will be added to you."

—Matthew 6:24, 33

Our Father, we confess that placing Jesus first in our lives precludes competition from all other loyalties: that no hobby or occupation or pursuit, however engaging, can contain all of our passion. No relationship, however intimate, can compete with Christ for first place in our hearts. No possession, however prized, can come between us and You.

Our Lord, we thank You for giving us our vocations—for the privilege of making a living. We're grateful for the place where we earn our wage and where we have the opportunity to live out our faith. May our work become a platform upon which Your Son, Jesus Christ, is placed on display day after day.

And our relationships, Father, how vital they are—how valuable! We place them before You as well.

May they be honoring to You. May they represent associations that model the glory of Jesus Christ rather than simply satisfy ourselves.

Regarding our ever-present battle with possessions — with things: we place on the altar all the "stuff" of our lives. Help us form our priorities, God. As we live in this physical world, help us put our possessions in their proper place, way down on the list of what's important . . . after You — after *all* relationships.

And so, Lord, we lay before You our work, our relationships, and our possessions. May they all be a part of the narrow path that leads us to the way of the cross.

We ask it in the name of Christ, our Lord. Amen.

See also Deuteronomy 6:5; Haggai 1:3 – 9;
Luke 8:14; 14:25 – 27; Philippians 3:8 –13.

STOP FUSSING . . . AND FOCUS INSTEAD

Mary . . . sat before the Master, hanging on every word he said. But Martha was pulled away by all she had to do in the kitchen. Later, she stepped in, interrupting them. "Master, don't you care that my sister has abandoned the kitchen to me? Tell her to lend me a hand." The Master said, "Martha, dear Martha, you're fussing far too much and getting yourself worked up over nothing. One thing only is essential, and Mary has chosen it."

—Luke 10:39–42 MSG

Father, we acknowledge that anxiety is not simply a worrisome little habit but rather, it is a sin . . . a repeated sin. Worry compromises our fellowship with You and with others. We thank You that the death of Your Son, Jesus, provided the payment in full for our sins, including the sin of worry. We trust Him to take care of our worries, just as the psalmist said, "Cast your burden upon the Lord and He will sustain you; He will never allow the righteous to be shaken."

We pray that You will quiet our hearts. As You do, please lead us to a quiet and sure confidence in Yourself. Take the things that we needlessly fuss over—those worries that have burdened us long enough—and erase them from our minds. Please teach us to focus on You instead—to sit at Your feet in quietness. And as we cast the heavy weight of anxiety on You, we will trust You to give us instead a peace that surpasses understanding and a confidence that You are at work—even though we remain in the same circumstances. Thank You ahead of time for how You will deal with the burdens that weigh heavily on our hearts. Thank You for how You will relieve the anxieties that cause us to miss the important things in life.

We thank You in the name of Christ our Lord and Savior. Amen.

See also Psalm 55:22; Proverbs 12:25; Isaiah 26:3; Matthew 6:31–34; Philippians 4:6–7; 1 Peter 5:7.

FOR FACING OUR OWN DEATH

"I am the resurrection and the life; he who believes in Me will live even if he dies, and everyone who lives and believes in Me will never die."

—John 11:25–26

Our Father, this is a sacred moment because we all must answer the question, "Am I ready to die?" And not until we're ready to die are we truly ready to live.

We acknowledge that death is the last thing we want to think about, but thank You for bringing us face-to-face with reality. Thank You for the gift of living on earth and the reminder that our days are fleeting. Make us ready for the harsh moments that are before us, calm our spirits, and remove our fears.

Thank You for Jesus Christ, who is the answer beyond the grave. This day, we acknowledge Him as Lord and Savior of life and death.

Now unto Him who is able to keep us from falling, and to present us faultless before the presence of His glory with exceeding joy, to the only wise God our Savior, be glory and majesty, dominion and power, both now and forever.

For Christ is risen indeed. In His name we pray. Amen.

See also Psalm 90:12; 116:15; Romans 8:23; Hebrews 9:27; Jude 1:24–25.

For Protection and Strength in the Face of Terrorism

"Cease striving and know that I am God;
I will be exalted among the nations, I will be
exalted in the earth."
*The L*ord *of hosts is with us;*
The God of Jacob is our stronghold.

—Psalm 46:10–11

O God, as never before in this generation, we are dependent upon You for protection and strength. Though the mountains quake, though bridges fall, though tunnels are destroyed, though ships sink, though there will be the loss of life, though there will be the threat of war, though there are even at this time terrorists and enemies within our midst, we will not fear. Our resolve is firm because our refuge lies in the eternal foundation of the living God.

We pray for parents. Strong and brave, may they stand. May they set their hearts on You for the protection of their offspring, especially those who serve in the military. We pray for loved ones and family members and friends who grieve the loss of those taken in terrorist acts and in fierce combat on the battlefield.

We pray that You will give our national leaders and their counselors great courage and wisdom. Give us sufficient trust and confidence to follow them. May our country and our world remain united as evil is assaulted and as we fall on our knees in humble repentance before You.

In the process of giving us victory, we pray that You will purge our nation. Bring us before You in humble trust and remind us over and over again that God is our refuge and strength, a very present help in trouble.

We ask this confidently in the name of Christ, our Victorious Warrior. Amen.

See also Psalm 46:1; 121:1–8; Matthew 10:28;
Romans 8:35–39; 1 Timothy 2:1–4.

FOR TURNING BITTERNESS INTO SWEETNESS

Even if you should suffer for the sake of righteousness, you are blessed. And do not fear their intimidation, and do not be troubled, but sanctify Christ as Lord in your hearts, always being ready to make a defense to everyone who asks you to give an account for the hope that is in you, yet with gentleness and reverence; and keep a good conscience so that in the thing in which you are slandered, those who revile your good behavior in Christ will be put to shame.

—1 Peter 3:14–16

Our Father, as we acknowledge Your Son as Lord over all, it is with a sigh, because we cannot deny the pain or ignore the difficulty of earthly trials. For some people the reality of this is borderline unbearable. But being sovereign and being the One with full capacity to handle our needs, You are strong enough to carry our burdens and, in return, to give us the perspective we need.

Quiet our spirits. Give us a sense of relief as we face the inevitable facts that life is difficult and that there will be those moments when life will not be at all fair. Erase any hint of bitterness. Enable us to see beyond the present, to focus on the invisible, and to recognize that You are always with us. Remind us, too, that Your ways are higher and far more profound than ours.

Thank You for the joy of this day. Thank You for the pleasure of a relationship with You and with a few good, caring, loving friends. And especially, Father, thank You for the truth of Your Word that lives and abides forever.

In the strong name of Him who is higher, Jesus the Lord, we pray. Amen.

See also Proverbs 14:19; 15:1; Ephesians 4:31–32; Hebrews 12:14–15; James 1:19–20.

Only for
the Lonely

Make every effort to come to me soon. . . .
Only Luke is with me. Pick up Mark and
bring him with you, for he is useful to me for
service. . . . At my first defense no one supported
me, but all deserted me; may it not be counted
against them. But the Lord stood with me and
strengthened me.

—2 Timothy 4:9, 11, 16–17

Our Father, we acknowledge that we need You, and our need is not partial; it's total. It's not occasional; it's always—today especially. We pray for those who wrestle with the very real problem of loneliness. It's not dated; it surfaces regularly in every generation. We pray especially for those who are lonely because they are distant from You. We ask You to bring them to a knowledge of Your Son and keep them restless and sleepless and struggling until they have come to that place of faith in Your Son.

Thank You for meeting our every need. We pray that You will meet this one today wherever we find ourselves. And that You will show Yourself strong where we are weak, mighty where we are lacking. Meet the deep needs of our hearts, our Father, and enable us to get through

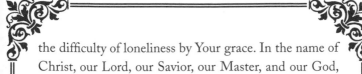

the difficulty of loneliness by Your grace. In the name of Christ, our Lord, our Savior, our Master, and our God, we pray. Amen.

See also Psalm 25:16−17; 68:6; 107:4−6.

FOR GENERATING A GENTLE SPIRIT

If we live by the Spirit, let us also walk by the Spirit. Let us not become boastful, challenging one another, envying one another. Brethren, even if anyone is caught in any trespass, you who are spiritual, restore such a one in a spirit of gentleness; each one looking to yourself, so that you too will not be tempted. Bear one another's burdens, and thereby fulfill the law of Christ.

—Galatians 5:25–6:2

We are very thankful, Father, that in the process of our spiritual growth You remind us of the importance of gentleness: Your Word not only instructs us in what we're to do, it also shows us how to do it. We remember what Paul wrote to the Thessalonians . . . he gently dealt with them as a mother with a nursing child. Help us, Father, to have that kind of gracious, gentle spirit—especially those of us who tend to be impatient with others who are not as quick on their feet . . . or those of us who are healthy and lack compassion for others who are not as strong . . . or those of us who find delight in accomplishments but lack empathy for others

who are not as productive. It's so easy for all of us—
if not verbally, at least in our minds—to compete, to
look down on others, to complain and to compare. May
we, through Your Spirit's power, become more like our
gentle Savior, who promised, "My yoke is easy and My
burden is light." Like our Master and Lord, may our
encounters with others be easy and bring light. Meet
our needs in a very special way, especially our need for a
gentle and quiet spirit.

In the name of Your gracious Son. Amen.

*See also Matthew 5:5; 11:29–30; Galatians 5:22–23;
1 Thessalonians 2:7.*

REMEMBERING THAT GOD IS FAITHFUL

Remember my affliction and my wandering,
*   the wormwood and bitterness.*
Surely my soul remembers
And is bowed down within me.
This I recall to my mind,
Therefore I have hope.
The LORD's lovingkindnesses indeed never
*   cease,*
For His compassions never fail.
They are new every morning;
Great is Your faithfulness.

                                        —Lamentations 3:19–23

Lord God, thank You for being more than a friend. Thank You for Your sovereign hand upon us, for Your mercies that are new every morning, for Your great faithfulness. Thank You for not leaving us when we should have been rejected and left, for not abandoning us when we deserved it. Thank You for being true to Your Word. Thank You for keeping Your promise that all who come to You will in no way be cast out. Thank You, our Shepherd, for Your sheepdogs—for goodness and mercy and, especially, faithfulness—

that follow unrelentingly at our heels. In faithfulness, You will receive those who come to You.

We pray for those who've run away from You. We request that You would win them back through Your compassion and mercy. We ask that they would sense the sympathetic faithfulness of God and that *that* alone would draw them like a magnet to You.

In the name of Christ, our strong Savior, we pray. Amen.

See also Numbers 23:19; Psalm 23:6; Zephaniah 3:5; John 6:37; Hebrews 10:23.

How to Begin a Relationship with God

Prayer is not a magic formula for persuading God to give us what we want. Praying isn't an incantation and it isn't hocus-pocus, but the Bible does make it clear that the "prayer of a person living right with God is something powerful to be reckoned with" (James 5:16 MSG). This, of course, assumes you are living right with God, because nowhere in the Scriptures does it say that God is under any obligation to answer the prayers of those who aren't living right with Him. So how do you get your life right with God, once and for all?

The answer to that question is not found in a prayer but in a Person—the person of God's Son, Jesus Christ, in whose name we pray. Because of Christ's sinless life, His painful death, and His glorious resurrection, all those who trust in Him can have their sins forgiven and receive eternal life. This kind of life is the right kind of life, and if you'd like to learn more about it, consider carefully the following essential truths.

Our Spiritual Condition: Totally Depraved

The first truth is rather personal. One look in the mirror of Scripture, and our human condition becomes painfully clear:

"There is none righteous, not
        even one;
There is none who understands,
There is none who seeks for God;
All have turned aside, together they
        have become useless;
There is none who does good,
There is not even one."
        (Romans 3:10 – 12)

We are all sinners through and through—totally depraved. Now, that doesn't mean we've committed every atrocity known to humankind. We're not as *bad* as we can be, just as *bad off* as we can be. Sin colors all our thoughts, motives, words, and actions.

If you've been around a while, you likely already believe it. Look around. Everything around us bears the smudge marks of our sinful nature. Despite our best efforts to create a perfect world, crime statistics continue to soar, divorce rates keep climbing, and families keep crumbling.

Something has gone terribly wrong in our society and in ourselves—something deadly. Contrary to how the world would repackage it, "me-first" living doesn't equal rugged individuality and freedom; it equals death. As Paul said in his letter to the Romans, "The wages of sin is death" (Romans 6:23)—our spiritual and physical death that comes from God's righteous judgment of our sin, along with all of the emotional and practical effects of this separation that we experience on a daily basis. This brings us to the second marker: God's character.

God's Character: Infinitely Holy

How can God judge us for a sinful state we were born into? Our total depravity is only half the answer. The other half is God's infinite holiness.

The fact that we know things are not as they should be points us to a standard of goodness beyond ourselves. Our sense of injustice in life on this side of eternity implies a perfect standard of justice beyond our reality. That standard and source is God Himself. And God's standard of holiness contrasts starkly with our sinful condition.

Scripture says that "God is Light, and in Him there is no darkness at all" (1 John 1:5). God is absolutely holy—which creates a problem for us. If He is so pure, how can we who are so impure relate to Him?

Perhaps we could try being better people, try to tilt the balance in favor of our good deeds, or seek out methods for self-improvement. Throughout history, people have attempted to live up to God's standard by keeping the Ten Commandments or living by their own code of ethics. Unfortunately, no one can come close to satisfying the demands of God's law. Romans 3:20 says, "By the works of the Law no flesh will be justified in His sight; for through the Law comes the knowledge of sin."

Our Need: A Substitute

So here we are, sinners by nature and sinners by choice, trying to pull ourselves up by our own bootstraps to attain a relationship with our holy Creator. But every time we try, we fall flat on our faces. We can't live a good enough life to make up for our sin, because God's standard isn't "good enough"—it's *perfection*. And we can't make amends for the offense our sin has created without dying for it.

Who can get us out of this mess?

If someone could live perfectly, honoring God's law, and would bear sin's death penalty for us—in our place—then we would be saved from our predicament. But is there such a person? Thankfully, yes!

Meet your substitute—*Jesus Christ*. He is the One who took death's place for you!

> [God] made [Jesus Christ] who knew
> no sin to be sin on our behalf, so that
> we might become the righteousness
> of God in Him. (2 Corinthians 5:21)

God's Provision: A Savior

God rescued us by sending His Son, Jesus, to die on the cross for our sins (1 John 4:9 – 10). Jesus was fully human and fully divine (John 1:1, 18), a truth that ensures His understanding of our weaknesses, His power to forgive, and His ability to bridge the gap between God and us (Romans 5:6–11). In short, we are "justified a gift by His grace through the redemption which is in Christ Jesus" (Romans 3:24). Two words in this verse bear further explanation: *justified* and *redemption*.

Justification is God's act of mercy, in which He declares righteous the believing sinners while we are still in our sinning state. Justification doesn't mean that God *makes* us righteous, so that we never sin again, rather that He *declares* us righteous—much like a judge pardons a guilty criminal. Because Jesus took our sin upon Himself and suffered our judgment on the cross, God forgives our debt and proclaims us PARDONED.

Redemption is Christ's act of paying the complete price to release us from sin's bondage. God sent His Son to bear His wrath for all of our sins—past, present, and future (Romans 3:24–26; 2 Corinthians 5:21). In humble obedience, Christ willingly endured the shame of the cross for our sake (Mark 10:45; Romans 5:6–8; Philippians 2:8). Christ's death satisfied God's righteous demands. He no longer holds our sins against us, because His own Son paid the penalty for them. We are freed from the slave market of sin, never to be enslaved again!

Placing Your Faith in Christ

These four truths describe how God has provided a way to Himself through Jesus Christ. Because the price has been paid in full by God, we must respond to His free gift of eternal life in total faith and confidence in Him to save us. We must step forward into the relationship

God that He has prepared for us—not by doing good works or by being a good person, but by coming to Him just as we are and accepting His justification and redemption by faith.

> For by grace you have been saved
> through faith; and that not of
> yourselves, it is the gift of God; not as
> a result of works, so that no one may
> boast. (Ephesians 2:8–9)

We accept God's gift of salvation simply by placing our faith in Christ alone for the forgiveness of our sins. Would you like to enter a relationship with your Creator by trusting in Christ as your Savior? If so, here's a simple prayer you can use to express your faith:

> *Dear God,*
>
> *I know that my sin has put a barrier between You and me. Thank You for sending Your Son, Jesus, to die in my place. I trust in Jesus alone to forgive my sins, and I accept His gift of eternal life. I ask Jesus to be my personal Savior and the Lord of my life. Thank You. In Jesus's name, amen.*

If you've prayed this prayer or one like it and you wish to find out more about knowing God and His plan for you in the Bible, contact us at Insight for Living. Our contact information is on the following pages.

WE ARE HERE FOR YOU

If you desire to find out more about knowing God and His plan for you in the Bible, contact us. Insight for Living provides staff pastors who are available for free written correspondence or phone consultation. These seminary-trained and seasoned counselors have years of experience and are well-qualified guides for your spiritual journey.

Please feel welcome to contact your regional Pastoral Ministries by using the information below:

United States
Insight for Living
Pastoral Ministries
Post Office Box 269000
Plano, Texas 75026-9000
USA
972-473-5097, Monday through Friday,
8:00 a.m. – 5:00 p.m. Central time
www.insight.org/contactapastor

Canada
Insight for Living Canada
Pastoral Ministries
Post Office Box 2510
Vancouver, BC V6B 3W7
CANADA
1-800-663-7639
info@insightforliving.ca

Australia, New Zealand, and South Pacific
Insight for Living Australia
Pastoral Care
Post Office Box 443
Boronia, VIC 3155
AUSTRALIA
1 300 467 444

United Kingdom and Europe
Insight for Living United Kingdom
Pastoral Care
PO Box 553
Dorking
RH4 9EU
UNITED KINGDOM
0800 915 9364
+44 (0) 1306 640156
pastoralcare@insightforliving.org.uk

RESOURCES FOR PROBING FURTHER

We hope that reading *The Prayers of Charles R. Swindoll* and making them your own have encouraged you not only in the specific areas in which Chuck prayed but also in deepening your own prayer life. Prayer is the surest measure for developing intimacy with God, so as you continue to draw closer to our Lord through prayer, we recommend the following resources. May they strengthen and freshen your own times of intimate communication with the Father.

Of course, we cannot always endorse everything a writer or ministry says, so we encourage you to approach these and all other non-biblical resources with wisdom and discernment.

Bounds, E. M. *Power through Prayer*. New Kensington, Pa.: Whitaker House, 1982.

Cowart, John W. *Why Don't I Get What I Pray For?* Downers Grove, Ill.: InterVarsity, 1993.

Getz, Gene A. *Praying for One Another*. Wheaton, Ill.: Victor Books, 1982.

Johnson, Jan. *When the Soul Listens: Finding Rest and Direction in Contemplative Prayer*. Colorado Springs: NavPress, 1999.

Maxwell, John. *Partners in Prayer: Support and Strengthen Your Pastor and Church Leaders*. Nashville: Thomas Nelson, 1996.

oth, Randall D. *Prayer Powerpoints*. Wheaton, Ill.: Victor Books, 1995.

Russell, Bob, with Rusty Russell. *When God Answers Prayer*. West Monroe, La.: Howard, 2003.

Swindoll, Charles R. *Intimacy with the Almighty: Encountering Christ in the Secret Places of Your Life*. Nashville: J. Countryman, 1999.

Swindoll, Charles R. "Prayer: Calling Out." In *Practical Christian Living: A Road Map to Spiritual Growth*. Compact Disc Series. Plano, Tex.: Insight for Living, 2008.

Swindoll, Charles R. *Simple Faith*. Nashville: Thomas Nelson, 2003.

Swindoll, Charles R. *When God Is Silent: Choosing to Trust in Life's Trials*. Nashville: J. Countryman, 2005.

Tada, Joni Eareckson. *Seeking God: My Journey of Prayer and Praise*. Brentwood, Tenn.: Wolgemuth & Hyatt, 1991.

Washington, James Melvin. *Conversations with God: Two Centuries of Prayers by African Americans*. New York: HarperCollins, 1994.

Webber, Robert. *The Book of Daily Prayer*. Grand Rapids: Eerdmans, 1993.

Wiersbe, Warren W. *Classic Sermons on Prayer*.
    Kregel Classic Sermons Series. Grand Rapids:
    Kregel, 1987.

Yancey, Philip. *Prayer: Does It Make Any Difference?*
    Grand Rapids: Zondervan, 2006.

ORDERING
INFORMATION

If you would like to order additional Insight for Living resources, please contact the office that serves you.

United States
Insight for Living
Post Office Box 269000
Plano, Texas 75026-9000
USA
1-800-772-8888 (Monday through Friday
7:00 a.m. – 7:00 p.m. Central time)
www.insight.org
www.insightworld.org

Canada
Insight for Living Canada
Post Office Box 2510
Vancouver, BC V6B 3W7
CANADA
1-800-663-7639
www.insightforliving.ca

Australia, New Zealand, and South Pacific
Insight for Living Australia
Post Office Box 443
Boronia, VIC 3155
AUSTRALIA
1 300 467 444
www.insight.asn.au

United Kingdom and Europe
Insight for Living United Kingdom
PO Box 553
Dorking
RH4 9EU
UNITED KINGDOM
0800 915 9364
www.insightforliving.org.uk

Other International Locations
International constituents may contact the U.S. office
through our Web site (www.insightworld.org), mail
queries, or by calling +1-972-473-5136.

SCRIPTURE INDEX

OLD TESTAMENT

SCRIPTURE INDEX

NEW TESTAMENT

SCRIPTURE INDEX

Scripture Index

Scripture Index

SUBJECT INDEX

SUBJECT INDEX

Subject Index

Subject Index